BHAGVAD GITA

A SONG SUNG BY GOD

*A free translation of the original Sanskrit text which
is a part of the Mahabharata*

Bhagvad Gita: A Song Sung by God

Raghupati Bhatt

Published in Melbourne, Australia.

BIC Classification:
HRG (Hinduism), HRGS (Hindu Sacred Texts).

978-0-9942525-8-6

NUMEN BOOKS
WWW.NUMENBOOKS.COM

Dedicated to Medha, my daughter, and Kiran, my son in law.

FOREWORD

This translation is a free translation. I might be wrong in places but I have written it as I understood it. It was a matter of great joy to be in the company of Shri Krishna and Arjuna. I straightaway entered the classical age and listened to their dialogue. I saw the universal form of Krishna. This is something unimaginable.

This is an uninterrupted work.

May Gita bless you.

Raghupati Bhatt

CONTENTS

ONE WHO DRINKS THIS NECTAR IS NEVER BORN AGAIN

Raghupati Bhatt

The Bhagvad Gita is a part of the *Mahabharata*, the most popular epic of India. It is a part of Bhishmaparva. The *Mahabharata* is the story of the feud between the sons of Dhrutrashtra and the sons of Pandu. Dhrutrashtra was born blind so Pandu was appointed king. Pandu was a valiant warrior but due to a curse he was unable to beget sons. He decided to renounce the kingdom and live life as a recluse. Dhrutarashtra became king, but Pandu could not father sons so his wives (he had two) received sons from the Gods. After a few years Pandu died and his wife Kunti came to Hastinapura along with her sons.

Dhrutrashtra had a hundred sons. The eldest was Duryodhana who did not like the arrival of these five strong contenders for the throne. He tried everything to eliminate the five brothers but every time he was unsuccessful. Finally he made the eldest of the Pandavas play a game of dice. With some clever moves he was successful in winning everything they had. He also insulted Draupadi, the wife of the Pandava brothers. Then the Pandavas were sent into exile. After going through all these ordeals the Pandavas returned and asked for their share. Duryodhana refused and the war became inevitable.

On the first day of war, when both the armies were facing each other, Arjuna wanted to have a look at the army so he told Shri Krishna to take the chariot into the middle of the battleground. When Arjuna saw his relatives ready to fight, he lost his nerve. Then Shri Krishna gave him some advice, which is called the *Bhagvad Gita*.

The *Bhagvad Gita* is an exposition on all the lines of thought prevalent in those times. The main idea is Sankhya. You can gain realization by a number of ways. Yoga is one of them, in which you do a number of physical exercises and awaken the latent power in yourself. Bhakti or devotion is another way in which you can surrender to God. There is also Dnyanyoga in which you can seek knowledge.

The *Bhagvad Gita* has eighteen chapters. Each chapter has a name which is very informative. For example, the first chapter is titled "Arjunvishadyoga", which means Arjuna's sadness. One chapter is called "Karmayoga" which means actions. Every chapter contains two lined verse which is called shloka. Most of the chapters are short. The second chapter however has seventy two verses. The last chapter is the longest of them all. It has seventy eight verses.

According to the *Mahabharata*, Dhrutrashtra wanted to know what was happening on the battleground. He was blind so his charioteer and friend Sanjay was granted a special vision by which he could see things happening on the battleground.

The book begins with the first verse "Dhrutrashtra Uwach." It means "Dhrutrashtra said".

Gita means a song. Bhagavat means the God. So this book is a song sung by the God. The book can actually be sung.

People have been reading or reciting the *Bhavad Gita* for several thousands of years. Outwardly, it looks simple but there are layers of meaning behind every word. Dnyaneshwara, who wrote a commentary on the *Bhagvad Gita*, explains the meaning of one shloka in several ovis - a meter in Marathi which has four lines. His explanation for one particular shloka is in eighty ovis. That explains how difficult the task of translating the *Bhagvad Gita* is. Dnyaneshwara did not create a mere translation. Dnyaneshwara has provided his own meaning. Aadi Shankaracharya also wrote a commentary on the *Bhagvad Gita* but it is in Sanskrit. Shankara too altered the meaning of the Gita. I do not know about translations in other languages.

In modern times Lokmanya Bal Gangadhar Tilak wrote a commentary on the *Bhagvad Gita* titled *Gita Rahasya*. Tilak is called the father of 'Indian Unrest' by Chirol. He interpreted the Gita according to his own ideology. Then there was Mahatma Gandhi who had deep faith in the *Bhagvad Gita*, and who also translated the *Bhagvad Gita*. His staunch disciple Vinoba Bhave translated it into Marathi with the title "*Geetaai*". He called the Gita 'aai' which means mother. There are many other translations. There is one by Swami Bhaktivedant Prabhupad, the founder of ISCON.

One Goan scholar D.D. Kosambi, who was Marxist in ideology, did not like the Gita because he felt that it was confusing. He had a different opinion about Shri Krishna also. But his views are not accepted by all.

There are many who think that the *Bhagvad Gita* was a later addition to the *Mahabharata*. To them even the character of Shri Krishna was an addition.

Whatever the opinions of the scholars might be, the *Bhagvad Gita* has been influencing the minds of people all over the world.

The Nobel laureate Oppenheimer had learnt the *Bhagvad Gita* by heart and when the first atomic explosion took place he described it with the help of a shloka from the *Bhagvad Gita*, "Like a thousand suns shining in the sky at the same time."

Swami Vivekananda had deep faith in the *Bhagvad Gita*. After his Guru's passing away he wandered through India. He was a monk and he kept with him only the most essential things. He had no money. Among the most essential things, he had kept two books. One was the *Imitation of Christ* by Thomas à Kempis and the other was the *Bhagvad Gita*. He felt that whenever he had any problems he would find the answer in the Gita.

For the ordinary man in India, the *Bhagvad Gita* has been a sacred thing. He is not bothered about its meaning. He or she feels immense joy in reciting it. The words have come from God.

The word 'man' that appears in the *Bhagvad Gita* refers to both genders. As Shri Krishna and Arjuna were both males it is the masculine gender that appears again and again. But one should interpret it as a common gender.

You can find everything in the Gita. You will find Marxism, Fascism, psychoanalysis, along with Christianity, Islam, Buddhism, Jainism, and many other religious faiths. But the main theme is the realization of God in man.

The Gita is not a Hindu scripture. Hinduism as it exists today was not in existence then. It is a universal religion that the Gita talks about. The word Dharma cannot be translated as religion. A teacher has to teach, or a warrior has to fight, or a king has to rule. These are their Dharmas according to the Gita. The Gita does not mention any of the Gods in the Hindu Pantheon, but talks about Brahma or the God principle. This Brahma is not the Brahmadeva of the Holy Trinity. It is the God, Allah, or The Almighty. It is about the main force behind this whole universe.

Krishna explains this using the first person I. He is not boasting. God is in each one of us. We have to realize that. Krishna was one such being who had understood this.

This is not a translation. It is an interpretation. I might be wrong in the interpretation, but I have tried my level best to make it as simple as possible. Many of the Sanskrit terms are literally untranslatable but I have tried my best. Even great people were at a loss when they tried to find the full meaning. My attempt is called Audhatya in Sanskrit which means 'irreverence' - Lord Shri Krishna will forgive me.

Dr. Iravati Karve felt that Shri Krishna literally lived the life he preached in the Gita. What he called "Nishkam Karmayoga", wherein one has to do his duties without worrying about the fruits of action, can be found in his life.

Let us now read Krishna's Karmayoga in his own words.

CHAPTER ONE

Dhrutrashtra, the blind father of the hundred Kauravas said to Sanjay, "On the sacred ground of Kurukshetra, in the company of the warriors, what did my sons and Pandu's son do Sanjay?"

Sanjay said, "When the King Duryodhana saw the Pandava army which was strategically arranged, he went to Dronacharya (the guru of both the Kauravas and Pandavas) and said,

"O master, look at this strategically placed army of the sons of Pandu, arranged by your wise disciple Dhrustadhymna.

In that army are many warriors who carry big bows like Bhima and Arjuna, Satyaki, Virat and Drupada, who are great charioteers. There are warriors Drishtaketu, Chekitan, mighty Kashiraj, Kuntibhoja and also a great man like Shaibya.

Valient Yudhamanyu, mighty Utamauja, and the five sons of Draupadi are also great warriors.

O great Brahmin, know about those chief warriors in our army. I am telling you about the chiefs in our army for your information.

You, Grandfather Bhishma, Karna, triumphant Krupacharya, also Ashwathhama, Vikarna and the son of Somadatta. There are many others, with many weapons who are ready to lay down their lives for me and who are well versed in battle techniques.

This army of ours protected by Grandfather Bhishma is unconquerable and their army, protected by Bhima, is easy to overcome.

So all of you get settled on different fronts and you will no doubt protect Grandfather Bhishma from all sides."

Then the oldest of the Kauravas, the valiant warrior, Grandfather Bhishma blew his conch like a lion's loud roar and created joy in the heart of Duryodhana.

After that conches, drums, and many other instruments created a huge noise which was terrible.

Then Shri Krishna and Arjuna, sitting in a fine chariot, drawn by white horses also blew their divine conches.

Shri Krishna's conch was "Panchajanya". Arjuna's was "Devadatta" and Bhima, who always did terrible deeds, blew a great conch called "Poundra".

The son of Kunti, King Yudhishtira, blew a conch called "Anantvijaya". Nakul and Sahdeva blew conches called Sughosha and Manipushpaka.

Kashiraj, who has a mighty bow, great charioteer Shikhandi, Dhrushtadhyumna, King Virata, unbeatable Satyaki, King Drupada, the five sons of Draupadi, Abhimanyu, the son of Subhadra with massive hands, all these people blew their conches, o King.

And that terrible noise shook the earth and sky, and frightened the sons of Dhrutrashtra.

13

Then, Arjuna, the one whose flag has a monkey on it, saw those standing sons of Dhrutrashtra, at the time of raising arms, raised his bow and said this to Shri Krishna, "Take my chariot between the two armies. I want to have a look at these war mongers and who I have to fight with in this conflict."

Sanjay said,

"Then when Arjuna spoke thus, Shri Krishna took the great chariot to the center between the two armies, in front of Bhishma and Drona and said, "Look at these assembled Kauravas."

After that Arjuna saw in both armies his grandfather, his master, uncles, brothers, sons, grandsons, friends, in-laws and many other dear ones.

When he saw all them, he had pity in his heart and mournfully he said,

"O Krishna, when I see these people who are willing to battle with me, my legs give up, my mouth has dried, and my body is shaking with goose pimples on it.

My bow "Gandiva" is falling from my hands, my skin is burning, my mind is confused, and I am finding it difficult to stand.

Krishna, I feel all these terrible symptoms. I don't see any good in killing my own people in this battle,

I don't want any victory in this battle. I want neither kingdom, nor any enjoyment. Why do we want this kingdom and what is the point of these pleasures in our life?

Those for whom we want this kingdom and joy are all standing here, after giving up all wealth and hope for life.

All these here are masters, elderly people, sons, grandfathers, maternal uncles, in-laws, grandsons, and other relatives.

O Madhusudan, even for the three kingdoms (earth, heaven and the underworld), I shall not kill people who are ready to use their arms against me. How can I kill them for this earth's kingdom?

Janardana, what pleasure can be achieved by killing these sons of Dhrutrashtra? We shall commit a sin by killing these sinners.

It is not right to kill these sons of Dhrutrashtra, who are my brothers. How can I be happy after killing my own people?

Even though these people have lost their reason because of greed and do not know what a great sin it is to destroy one's own clan or to betray one's own friends, we know that so why shouldn't we avoid this?

When the clan is destroyed, the traditions and rites die, and then this wrong engulfs all the clan.

Then the women-folk are affected which leads to the mixing of clans.

Then those destroyers of the clan and the traditions are the causes of hell, and because there are no funeral rites, even the ancestors are dragged into hell.

We have heard from sages that these destroyers of the clan and traditions definitely go to hell. To attain a kingdom we have become ready to slay our own people.

Even if these armed sons of Dhrutrashtra kill me, who am not resisting and am without arms on the battle ground, it will be better for me."

15

Sanjay said,

"Thus saying, Arjuna whose mind was troubled with grievous thoughts gave up his bow and arrows and sat down in the rear of the chariot."

In this way the first chapter of the Bhagvad Gita, which is a theology, Upanishad and science of yoga consisting of a dialogue between Shri Krishna and Arjuna which is called Arjunvishadyoga (Arjuna's Sadness) ends.

CHAPTER TWO

Sanjay said,

"Then Madhusudan (Shri Krishna) said this to Arjuna who was very sad and full of tears."

Shri Bhagvan said,

"How has this unbecoming sentiment for Aryas, one that gives disrepute to great men, visited you at such a crucial time?

Partha, do not be gutless, this weakness is not befitting to the likes of you. Give up this weakness and rise up."

Arjuna said,

"Madhusudana, how can I shoot my arrows at Bhishma and Drona, both of whom are worth worshiping?

It is better to beg than to kill great masters. If I kill my master, my gains will be stained with blood which is detestable.

I don't know what is better. I don't know whether we shall win or they. I don't want to kill these sons of Dhrutrashtra, who are confronting us, and live.

I, because of the vice of cowardice, and confusion about my duties, ask you what is better for me because I am your disciple and so have come to you. Give me knowledge.

Because even after winning this kingdom and becoming master of the celestial beings, I do not see any solution for the sadness which has dried my senses."

Sanjay said,

"O King, Arjuna who has conquered sleep said this to Shri Krishna and declared that he would not fight and became quiet.

O born in Bharat clan, then Shri Krishna, who lives in everybody's heart, smilingly said this to the grief stricken Arjuna."

Shri Bhagvan said,

"You are grieving for those who do not deserve it, and wise men say that the wise do not grieve either for the dead or for the living.

It is not that I was not present at any time, or you were not present, or these kings were not present. It is not so that we shall not be there in future.

This body has childhood, youth and old age similarly; there is a new body so the wise men are not tempted by this.

O son of Kunti, these organs give us pleasure and pain through cold and warmth, which is but temporary, so bear with them.

O superior man, those who regard pleasure and pain as the same, and who are not disturbed by sensory things are right for salvation.

The untrue is never there and the true is never missing. Such is seen by the philosophers.

That one which has filled this world is indestructible. Nobody is able to kill the indestructible.

The soul is incomparable and is eternal, but the body is perishable - so Arjuna do fight.

Those who think that the soul kills and those who think that the soul is killed, both do not know that the soul nether kills, nor gets killed.

This soul was never born in any time and is never dead, because the soul is unborn and eternal. Even if the body perishes, the soul remains.

O son of Prutha, one who knows that the soul is immortal, unborn and without any end, neither kills anybody nor causes anybody to be killed.

When one's cloth is worn out, one gives it up and obtains a new one, similarly when one's body becomes old, the soul living in this body gives it up and wears a new one.

Weapons cannot cut this soul. Fire cannot burn it. Water cannot wet it nor wind can dry it. It is inseverable, incombustible, unwettable and undriable. It is everywhere, like a tree trunk it is unmovable and eternal.

This soul is abstract; you cannot think about it, nothing affects it so it is not right for you to grieve over it.

Even if you think that the soul is born and it dies, o valiant Arjuna it is not right for you to grieve over it.

One who is born is sure to die and one who is dead is sure to be born again, so you should not grieve over such inevitable things.

All beings are without body before they are born. As long as they are alive they have bodies and after death they exist without body.

So why grieve over such things?

Some see this soul with wonder, some talk about it in wonder. Some hear about it in wonder, but still they do not know about it.

Arjuna, this soul which resides in the body cannot be killed so it is not right to grieve over it.

When you know your duties, this kind of hesitation does not suit you. For a warrior nothing is better than war.

This war is a heaven's gate opened by providence to you and only a few lucky warriors receive such an opportunity.

If you do not fight this just war, it will be a sin which will deprive you of your reputation.

Everybody will talk about your dishonor, and for gentlemen dishonor is worse than death.

These warriors will say that you ran away because of fear. So far they regard you as a great warrior, but now they will come to despise you.

They will say petty things about your prowess. Is anything sadder than this?

If you die fighting, you will go to heaven and if you win, you will reign over all the earth, so decide and get up and fight.

Regard pleasure and pain as the same; victory and defeat as the same and fight. There is no sin then.

I told you about the reason given by theology. Now listen on how to attain that state so that you can free yourself from the shackles of action.

If you follow this path, your actions will remain intact and there is no fault in it. Even if you practice a little of this path, you will be saved from the consequences.

Those who are decided, have only one path before them. Those who are undecided, find many paths before them.

Those who are engaged in finding the meaning of Vedas, those for whom the sensual pleasures are very important, those who talk about how to gain wealth and pleasures, for whom their fruits of action are like a flowering tree, and thus these minds are lost to sensual pleasures and cannot decide on the right path.

Small ponds serve the same purpose as big lakes. (If you are surrounded by water, you do not care about the small ponds.) Similarly, whatever you get out of the Vedas is also available in the deeds of a wise Brahmin.

Your right is to do your duties. You should never bother about their outcome. Do not seek the fruits of action and never think about inaction.

Dhananjaya, give up the desire for the fruits, do not consider the positive or negative outcome and do your duties. This balancing is called yoga.

Dhananjaya, this balanced act is better. Those deeds, done with desiring the fruits are worse. Seek knowledge. Those who are desirous are ignorant.

Those wise men who renounce the fruits of pleasure and the pain of actions are freed from the shackles of birth and death and reach that eternal state where there is no disturbance.

When you exit this swamp of temptation then you will attain that knowledge that is bestowed in the scriptures.

When your mind is freed, all the confusion ends and you become totally content in yourself, you achieve that yoga state."

Arjuna said,

"Keshava, what are the traits of such self content, of one whose mind is settled in oneself (sthitapradnya)? How does he talk? How does he live? How does he behave?"

Shri Bhagavan said,

"Partha, when a person gives up all his desires and is content, he is called sthitapradnya.

One who is not affected by mishaps, or has no desires left for the good things, one who has no affection, anger, or fear is called Sthitapradnya.

One who has no feelings towards other creatures, one who is not congratulating on auspicious things, nor hating the inauspicious things, has his mind settled.

As the tortoise is resigned to its shell, when a being renounces all his sensory perceptions and is resigned to one's self, his mind is settled.

Those who cannot enjoy sensual pleasures, such as weak and starving people, also are fond of such pleasures but the sthitapradnyas experience even sensual pleasures with God as realization and resignation.

O son of Kunti, even the minds of wise people who are trying, are lost in sensual pleasures by force.

One who controls his sensory organs, and is very calm, and for whom nothing is superior to me, has his mind settled in himself.

Concentration on pleasure creates love of pleasure. Because of love, desire is created, and from desire anger is born.

Anger creates irrationality. Irrationality breeds loss of memory, which in turn slays reason, and following the loss of reason, the person is lost.

One who has full control over his sensory organs and experiences pleasures through them, one who has his mind in reign, is qualified for contentment of mind.

This contentment destroys all evils and this pleasant state of mind and intelligence is quickly settled, so one should enjoy pleasures of the senses which are not forbidden and which are essential.

One whose mind is not settled, does not know about the soul, and does not have the sense that he is the eternal being, does not obtain peace of mind, and how can one be happy without peace of mind?

One who is involved in sensual pleasures, and who does not know about the soul, his reason is driven away by his mind like a boat in water is driven away by the wind.

So Arjuna, one who has kept his sensory organs under control and has kept away from sensual pleasures has his mind settled.

When it is night for all beings, the yogi remains awake and when it is daytime for all others, for the wise man it is night.

As the sea is undisturbed when water from the rivers enters from all sides, the desires which enter the mind of the sthitapradnya do not disturb him at all as he has peace of mind. The people who desire are never at peace.

One who gives up all desires, is without any affection, and one who does his duties without any selfish interest, obtains peace of mind.

Even after reaching that state, one who is not tempted remains in that state when the end comes and he reaches the eternal state."

Thus ends the second chapter of Bhagvad Gita, which is a theology, Upanishad and science of yoga, in the form of a dialogue between Shri Krishna and Arjuna titled "Saankhyayoga" (The Yoga of Equality).

CHAPTER THREE

Arjuna said,

"Krishna, if you think that knowledge and reason are superior to actions and deeds, why are you instigating me to violence? By uttering these confusing sentences you are tempting me and making me indecisive. You decide on one course which is better for me and tell me."

Shri Bhagvan said,

"Innocent Arjuna, in this world, there are two kinds of states. Earlier the Vedas proclaimed ritualistic state. Then knowledgeable people spoke about the sthitpradnyas and the state of action was professed for those whose abilities are not strong.

Those who are wise, unless they begin with rituals, are not eligible for the state of knowledge. Even if they renounce without knowledge, they cannot reach that state of knowledge.

Because no one can remain devoid of actions, for every being has to do certain things assigned by the Creator, through the three qualities ascribed to all.

One who controls his sensory organs but thinks about the pleasures is called a hypocrite.

Arjuna, one who controls his sensory organs, has control over one's mind, and performs his work without expecting the fruits, is a superior being.

The usual duties have to be performed. This is better than not doing anything. If one does not do the usual tasks, the body also cannot attain that perfect state.

One who performs other actions than those done for self realization, is bound to those other things. So Arjuna - give up the desire for fruits and act for self realization.

In the beginning, Brahma, the creator, created the three upper classes and gave them the fire ritual and said to them, "With this fire, develop yourself. Let this fire grant you whatever you wish."

You can please Indra (the supreme God in the Vedas) by this fire that in turn will help you to develop. Helping each other to grow will then entitle you to reach that highest goal of realization through knowledge.

When you give the gods their share of pleasures, they will be pleased and will give you whatever pleases you. Those who do not give their share to the gods are thieves.

Those who eat the remains, after giving the shares to the gods through fire rituals, are absolved of all sins. Those who only cook food for filling their stomach are sinners.

Whatever food is eaten by beings makes their bodies. The food is created by rain. The rain is created by fire. The fire is created by the actions of the host and the priests engaged in fire rituals. The actions are created by Brahma, and Brahma is born of the Word. So this whole universe is the manifestation of Brahma and is eternal, ever bright and is settled in the fire.

This cycle is created by Brahma, and those who are not following this and are engaging in sensual pleasures, live in vain.

On the other hand, one who is content in one's soul, has no duties to perform.

If he does something there is no effect from it and if he does not do anything, nothing matters. This knowledge has not been resorted to by anybody.

So give up your desires and do the work assigned to you. Those who give up their desires and do their work with dedication to God gain salvation.

Wise warriors like Janaka performed their duties and finally achieved realization. A person like you, who always cares for other people so that they do not stray, is the right person to act.

Whatever the great man does is followed by his disciples and followers. All other people try to behave like that great man.

Arjuna, for me there are no duties in all the three worlds. I have not achieved anything and there is nothing to achieve for me, and even then I continue to do my duties.

Because if I neglect and do not do my duties, other people will follow my example and do the same.

If they do not do their duties, they will perish, and then I shall be responsible for the deaths of those people.

The foolish people do their duties with the assumption that they are doing them, and they would definitely obtain the fruits of the action. Wise men who want to gather men around them should do their duties without both that assumption and any desire for fruits.

One should not disturb the people who are engaged in actions and seek fruits of action. One should not move them away from their actions. Wise men keep their minds calm, do their duties and get their work done by this.

One who because of ego, thinks that he does all the things which are the consequences of nature and her demands from the body.

On the other hand one who knows about the qualities, sections, and sensory organs, knows that the demands of the body are converted into desires and so is unaffected.

The ignorant think that whatever movement occurs due to desires, are undertaken for the fruits of action. The wise men should not try to change them.

Those devotees who worship me and do their duties devotedly are absolved by me of good deeds or sins.

On the other hand those who are not following my advice and are not behaving properly, are ignorant fools who are lost.

Even the wise man does all the things as per his disposition. All living beings act according to their disposition. One should not be attracted or detached to sense-objects because they both block his progress.

Doing one's duty is advisable even though it has less merits. Even death while doing one's duty is preferrable and brings good fruits. The other's duties are detestable."

Arjuna said,

"Shri Krishna, is such a man provoked by somebody, unwillingly, as if forced to take the wrong path?"

Shri Bhagwan said,

"A person is provoked to do wrong by desire and anger, which are very demanding. Both of them are evil and are produced by a middle disposition called Rajasa. Regard this desire as your enemy.

As the smoke obscures the fire, the fetus is obscured with water, or the mirror is obscured by dust, the soul is obscured by desire and anger.

Arjuna, this desire is the enemy of the wise man, which never says enough, and has eclipsed knowledge.

This desire resides in our sensory organs. Through the organs this desire makes one proud of his body, and eclipsing this knowledge, goes on tempting the being.

Arjuna, give up this evil desire by controlling your sensory organs, for they are the destroyer of knowledge.

Wise men say that the five sense organs are better than the rest of the body. The mind is superior to the bodily organs. Intelligence is still more superior, and the soul is the supreme.

So Arjuna, know this about the true nature of your soul, control this desire with the help of your mind, and eliminate that desire."

Thus ends the third chapter of Bhagvad Gita, theology, Upanishad and science of yoga, in the form of a dialogue between Shri Krishna and Arjuna called "Karmayoga" (The Yoga of Action).

CHAPTER FOUR

Shri Bhagavan said,

"I gave this eternal knowledge to the Sun god, who gave it to Manu, the first man. Manu told it to his son Ikshwaku.

This knowledge was thus passed to future generations by the kings. They practiced it. A lot of time has passed, so this knowledge has no followers.

I have told you about this ancient knowledge because you are my disciple, my friend, and because this knowledge is the best."

Arjuna said,

"We were born a few years ago. The Sun was born in the beginning. You say that you gave this knowledge to the Sun. How can I believe it to be true?"

Shri Bhagvan said,

"Arjuna, I and you have had a number of births. I know these different lifetimes, I remember them. But you don't know and you don't remember.

Though I am beyond birth and death and am eternal in nature, and though I control this universe, sometimes I use my illusion of three qualities, and am born, appearing to be human.

Arjuna, whenever that which is right is on the decline and that which is wrong is on the rise, I take birth.

Arjuna, to protect the good and to destroy the evil, I appear in every age.

Arjuna, those who know about my extraordinary birth and work, are freed from the cycle of life, are not reborn after death, and reach me in the end.

Those who are without affection, fear or anger, become absorbed in me and surrender to me, have reached my state with their knowledge and penance.

Those who worship me are blessed by me. No matter how they worship me. The wise men, who know this, follow my path.

Those who want fruits of their action worship the deities and get the fruits immediately.

I have created four classes of people according to their qualities and work, but know that I am both the creator and also a non creator.

I do not desire fruits of action, so actions do not affect me. Those who know this are also freed from the effects of action.

The earlier enlightened souls have known about this and have acted accordingly, so you too, do your duties like them.

Even the wise are confused about what is to be done and what is not to be done. I shall tell you the principle of action, knowing which will free you from worldly things.

We should know the nature of the action and inaction, and also the wrong act because these acts are very confounding.

One who sees inaction in the acts, and action in the inaction, is both a wise man and a yogi who does everything.

One who does everything without any desire or aim, and has thus burnt all actions is called a knowledgeable one.

That person is unworldly, is content in his own self, and does his work without any desire for fruit or that false assumption that he is inactive despite his actions.

One who has his mind and body under control, one who has not anything to store, if he performs essential body functions, there is no sin in that.

One who does not beg but is content in whatever he receives, is not affected by cold or heat, is not bothered by pleasure or sorrow, has no jealousy, does not hate anybody, and without thinking about success or failure does his duty, is not bound by those actions.

One free from desire, one who is always in pursuit of knowledge, who performs his duties with the mind settled, is freed from all restraints of action. One who is without attachments, who seeks truth and works for the fire sacrifice gets his actions burnt in that.

Whatever is sacrificed is God, the matter to be burnt is God. In the fire named God, the sacrificed is God and whatever fruits are there, go to God.

Other yogis do this fire ritual methodically, but the wise men think of God as fire, the combustible as God, and perform the ritual.

Some think of their sensory organs as being flammable in the fire of control. Some burn the word in the fire of sensory organs, which means they listen to the demands of their bodies and with no desire, affection burns their actions to ashes.

Those who give money to the right people are performing the fire ritual of money. Those who do penance are performing the fire ritual of penance.

Those in yoga are performing the fire ritual of yoga. Those who are studying Vedas are performing the fire ritual of knowledge. Finally, those who resort to the most difficult methods by renouncing everything are those who possess knowledge of the eternal truth.

Some do the fire ritual by merging the outgoing with the incoming breath and after controlling the speed of both, perform pranayama, (control of breath).

Some take little food, control their breaths and conduct the fire ritual. Those who know about these rituals burn the effects of their deeds.

After performing the fire ritual, in the remaining time they imbibe ambrosia and reach the eternal state. Those who are not doing fire rituals do not reach even the present desirable state, and how can they think of any higher state?

These are the different kinds of fire rituals spread from the Vedas. After knowing about them and the actions, you will be freed from these worldly affairs.

Arjuna, the best is the fire ritual of knowledge. All actions finally end up in knowledge.

You go to the Gurus, prostrate before them, ask questions to them and acquire this knowledge. You serve them and those philosophers will give knowledge to you.

Once you acquire this knowledge, you will not be confused and will see in all creatures, as well as in yourselves, me - the Eternal Principle.

Even if you are the most evil character doing the worst things, this vessel of knowledge will definitely take you to the other side.

Arjuna, as the well-lit fire burns all the wood and turns it to ash, this fire of knowledge burns the effects of your action.

There is nothing in this world which is as sacred as this knowledge. One who does his duties has this equality in his mind, in course of time, obtains this knowledge of self automatically.

One who has faith, and control over his sensory organs, achieves this knowledge. After that he receives salvation very soon.

One who does not know about the soul and one who has no faith is lost. He does not receive anything in this world and does not receive anything in the afterworld.

Arjuna, one who knows the soul and God to be one and has no doubts in his mind, and has given up both right and wrong, such an alert being is not bound by actions.

So sever this doubt, confusion, and temptation born out of ignorance, with the sword of knowledge - be ready for action Arjuna and rise up for war."

Thus ends the fourth chapter of Bhagvad Gita which is a theology, Upanishad and science of yoga in the form of a dialogue between Shri Krishna and Arjuna which is called "Dnyankarma sanyasyoga" (The Yoga of Knowledge, Action, and Renunciation).

CHAPTER FIVE

Arjuna said,

"Krishna, you tell me to renounce karma and again you tell me to do the rituals - so decide which is better for me and tell me."

Shri Bhagvan said,

"For the one who is seeking realization both doing action and renouncing action are equal and they take him to his desired end. But taking action is definitely better than inaction.

One who does not either hate or desire anything is a monk because, o valiant Arjuna, one who does not have divided feelings is automatically liberated.

Ignorant people think that renunciation and yoga produce different kinds of fruit, but the wise can use any one of them and produce the desired result.

Whatever is achieved through equal practice is achieved by the yogis in due course of time. So one who sees that equality, knowledge and devotion towards knowledge, yoga, and enacting duties without the desire for fruits of action are one, both see the right and both know the right.

Arjuna, achieving total renunciation without equilibrium is very difficult. The wise man who follows the rituals provided in the Vedas and seeks God, achieves his aims very soon.

One who follows this and does his duties without seeking the fruit of action, whose mind is very pure and who has his body and organs under control, becomes one with the Eternal Principle residing in all creatures and then no deed can bind him.

The wise man thinks that he is not looking through his eyes, not hearing with his ears, not feeling with his skin, not smelling through his nose, nor tasting with his tongue. One who walks and sleeps with his mind surrendered, who breathes, talks with speech organs, accepts with hands, passes urine and stools, closes and opens his eyelids, enjoys all the pleasures with the assumption that he is not the doer has his mind fixed in the soul.

One who does his duties, dedicates them to God and gives up the desire for the fruits of action, is like the leaf of a lotus which is not wet despite being in water, and is not affected by his deeds.

Those yogis perform their duties either physically or mentally, or through sensory organs, without any desire, only to purify their body and mind through routine activities.

One who is a seeker of the eternal truth thinks that he is doing so for God and not for himself, obtains peace of mind. Those who are disturbed have desires and those who are seeking the fruits of action, are bound by their actions.

The conqueror of organs, with the soul residing in this body, does not use the nine orifices of this body, does nothing himself or does not get anything done lives peacefully.

The soul has no duties for people, never creates anything, and is not related to anything, this is all the doing of ignorance and illusion.

The all pervading soul does not take the sin of anybody or the fruits of good deeds of anybody. The conscience is eclipsed by ignorance which tempts living beings.

If ignorance is destroyed with this knowledge, knowledge brightens the soul like the sun.

Those, always engaged in the God principle, have become like that, have loyalty in that, are interested only in that, and those whose sins have been destroyed because of knowledge, are never born again and reach the final state.

In the unassuming Brahmin who has knowledge, in the cow, elephant, dogs, or in the lowest of the servants, the wise men see the same God Principle.

One who sees this God Principle in all living beings has conquered his next birth, because the God Principle is indestructible and flawless, and is the same everywhere in which they are always engaged.

After obtaining desires, he is not delighted, after experiencing the worst, he is not sad. His mind is settled and he has no doubt that the God Principle is the same and flawless. Such a soul is all knowing and is in the God Principle.

His mind is never on worldly things like words. He experiences the joy of the God Principle. He is totally merged with this so he experiences joy without end.

Because the pleasures obtained from sensory organs are the seeds of future sorrow. They are born and they die, so Arjuna, wise men do not indulge in these pleasures.

One who can control the pace of sensuality and anger before the demise of the body is a yogi and is a happy man.

One who finds pleasures in one's soul, amusement in the soul, light in the soul, and becomes one with his soul, reaches the God Principle in the end. One who has done little wrong, has no doubts and is engaged in the welfare of all living beings, finally reaches the God Principle.

The yogi with the mind that knows neither sensuality nor anger, whose mind is fully under control, he reaches salvation whilst alive and remains in that state after death.

He that keeps the worldly subjects like words, touch, etc. out and continues concentrating on the center of his brows, controlling his breath, and has his organs under control, is a free being.

By penance and fire ritual, knowing me who runs this world, and helping all without any expectations, one gains immense peace."

Thus ends the fifth chapter of Bhagvad Gita, which is a theology, Upanishad and science of yoga, in the form of a dialogue between Shri Krishna and Arjuna called Karmasanyasyoga (Renouncing the Actions).

CHAPTER SIX

Shri Bhagvan said,

"One who does his rituals regularly as a duty without any desire for the fruits, is a yogi and a monk. He is not a non-doer or a non-performer of rituals. You cannot call a mere non-doer or performer a yogi or monk.

Arjuna, call it a renunciation which is defined by scriptures. One who has a desire cannot become a yogi.

One who wants to practice meditation has to do his deeds without any desire. Afterwards when he becomes adept, he is advised to renounce actions altogether.

When the yogi has lost his interest in the pleasures of his body, has resigned from his actions, he is said to be a rider on yoga.

The soul should liberate the soul, it should not be the cause of the downfall of the soul. Because the soul is the brother of the soul, and soul itself is the enemy of the soul.

One who conquers his body knows that his soul is his friend. One who has not conquered his body, has his soul active in enmity.

One who has conquered oneself and so has the mind in a blissful state, his soul becomes one with God and lives like that Eternal Principle, and experiences heat and cold, happiness and sorrow, honor or insult, in the same way. He comes to know about the nature of things in a scientific way, so is unmoved by any situation and becomes the conqueror of his organs. Such a soul, for whom gold and dust are the same is called the right man.

He is a friend who helps without any expectations, without taking any side, naturally thinks about the welfare of the enemy and the friend, regards the saints and the sinners as the same, this is the best man.

One who is meditating, sitting in a secluded place, controlling both body and mind, has no thirst, and has not stored anything, should always keep his mind calm and settled.

He should sit in a pious place which is neither high nor deep, on a piece of a deer skin or tiger skin over grass. There should be a soft cloth over it.

Once he sits there, he should control his mind and body, and start meditating to purify the mind with full concentration.

The head, the torso, and the neck should be in one line, and the yogi should gaze at the tip of his nose, and should not look anywhere else.

One whose mind is very calm, without any fear, and is celibate, is devoted to me and thinks about me.

Such a yogi who keeps his mind in such a pleasant state meditates, reaches salvation, and finally obtains that peace which is under my control.

This yoga cannot be practiced by people who eat more than enough. Those who eat very little also cannot practice. Those that sleep too much cannot practice. And those who have little sleep cannot practice this yoga.

When the controlled mind concentrates on the soul, the yogi eliminates all desires, visible and invisible actions, and he has no desire either for worldly or heavenly pleasures, he is called the right man.

Such a mind engaged in yoga, which is calm and settled, can be compared with the undisturbed burning wicker of a lamp in a windless region.

With the practice of yoga one controls his mind from all sides, looks at the God with his pious mind, and delights. Then he enjoys the bliss which cannot be enjoyed by body organs and only through the intellect. When he is settled in this state and is unmoved, he receives the benefits of that state.

This attainment is higher than any other thing and if you believe this, no sorrow whatever might be the nature of it, can disturb you.

One who is in this state where the sorrows melt, is called the knower of yoga. This yoga is to be practiced with determination.

All the actions where desire is at the root are to be abandoned without exception.

Control your organs with a conscious mind; courageously merge your mind with your soul at a steady pace. Don't think of anything else. The mind is very difficult to control so avoid subjects like words and control. This state is called conquering oneself.

One whose mind is very calm and who has no temptation, who is merged in the Eternal Principle, one who never does a wrong thing, such a yogi gets tremendous bliss.

In this order, one with a controlled mind, flawless, a regular practitioner of yoga, who is close to the Eternal Principle, enjoys eternal bliss.

The mind filled with yoga, sees the same everywhere, sees him in all creatures, sees me in all creatures, is never away from my sight or I am never away from his sight.

One who worships me in all creatures reaches me in the end, no matter how he behaves.

Arjuna, one who feels the pleasure and pain of all beings is the supreme yogi."

Arjuna said,

"Madhusudana (Krishna), because of my fickle mind, I cannot see this yoga of equality which is as steady as you have told me. Because the mind is very unsteady, it makes the body and organs very agitated, very uncontrollable, and cannot be penetrated. I think the control of the mind is difficult, like controlling the wind."

Shri Bhagvan said,

"Arjuna, there is no doubt that it is difficult to control this fickle mind, but constant practice and renunciation can make it possible.

I think that, for one whose mind is difficult to penetrate, due to renunciation and practice, for him this yoga is difficult. But for the yogi who has his mind under control, it can be easily achieved."

Arjuna said,

"Krishna, what happens to those who do not try, who are respectful towards this yoga, but in the end are strayed from it, what is their predicament? Those who have strayed from rituals and also renunciation, those without shelter like a lone cloud, do they perish? Only you can clear this doubt. No one else can do it."

Shri Bhagvan said,

"Arjuna, those who follow the right path never perish either in this world or the afterworld. Because my friend, the followers of the right path never go down.

One who has strayed from yoga enters the heaven where good people live. He lives in that world for a long time and is then transferred to the world where the rich people who follow the right path live.

Or he is born again in the family of intelligent but poor people. Taking birth in such family is also very difficult. He gains his lost knowledge there, and because of the practice of his previous birth he tries to reach greater heights.

With his practice he obtains what has been unattainable to him. He goes beyond the Word (the Vedas).

One who goes on practicing and whose bad deeds are washed away, goes on practicing for many life times and finally is liberated.

He is superior to the sages who perform very difficult types of penance. The yogi is superior to the learned pundits. The yogi is superior to the people who perform fire rituals. So Arjuna, be a yogi.

He is superior to other yogis who worship another deity. The devoted yogi who concentrates on me and worships me with devotion is very dear to me."

Thus ends the sixth chapter of the Bhagvad Gita which is a theology, Upanishad and science of yoga, in the form of a dialogue between Shri Krishna and Arjuna and is called "Abhyasyoga" (The Science of Practicing).

CHAPTER SEVEN

Shri Bhagvan said,

"Arjuna, you who are drawn towards me, take resort in me, you practice yoga, you are a man of all qualities, you will understand so listen. I shall speak to you with experience and examples of this knowledge, and there is nothing better than this to know.

One among thousands of people tries to access this knowledge; among thousands of knowledge seekers, perhaps only one knows me in a real sense.

The sense of smell, the sense of taste, the sense of touch, the principle of sight, the word, the mind, the ego, the reason of this, the eternal principle - are my manifestations through illusion.

Arjuna, this nature is inferior to my nature which is manifest in both the living and the non-living. This nature is mega-nature. It is there in the entire universe.

The whole universe is created from these two things. They are the cause of all that is living and non-living. I create this universe and I destroy it.

Arjuna, there is nothing superior to me. As the beads are woven in one thread, the whole universe is woven into me.

Arjuna, I am the liquid in water bodies. I am the brightness of the sun and the moon. In the Vedas I am the first letter Om (the sound Om is regarded as the first sound). In space I am the word. In men I am the masculinity.

I am the scent of the earth, and I am the glare of the fire. In all living beings I am the life force. For those who do penance, I am the penance in them.

Arjuna, know me as the eternal seed of all things. I am the reason in intelligent people. I am the charisma in the charismatic people. I am the might of the mighty, without any thirst or desire. Arjuna, I am the desire of all creatures who abide by the laws and scriptures.

The good, the average, and the bad are all born of me. I am not in them - they have no control over me - but they are under my control.

This universe is made up of these three qualities and because of desire, temptation, and jealousy, people are confused and hence do not know me, who is beyond these qualities, eternal and very splendid.

Because of my illusion these three qualities are very difficult to overcome. Those who surrender to me can do this.

The sinners, whose knowledge is eclipsed by my illusion, the people who are demonic and very wicked, do not surrender to me. I have four kinds of devotees who worship me. One who is in trouble, one who is a seeker of knowledge, one who wants wealth, and the fourth is one who wants to know God.

Among these four, I prefer most the one who is a seeker of knowledge, one whose mind is settled in me, and one who believes in one God because they are like me and I am like them.

All these four are very good, but the seeker of truth is my soul, for after concentrating on me they will reach me.

After many lifetimes one who has realized the truth, one who knows that everything is Vasudeva (Vasudeva is Krishna's name), comes to me in the end. Such a soul is very rare.

Those who have lost their reason due to different desires are controlled by their desire, and following this, they take resort in others.

If one desires to worship another, I keep their desires and their faith intact.

He worships that other, and receives the fruits which I have created through that other.

Those whose reasoning is very poor, obtain fruits which are perishable. Those who worship others reach those others. My devotees come to me.

Those ignorant people do not know about my eternal and grand nature and think that I, who was never born and has no form, am manifest now.

Eclipsed by my illusion, I am not manifest to all, not visible to all. I am unborn and without any attachments, but for these fools I become unknowable.

Arjuna, I know all who were in the past, who are now, and who will be in future - but nobody knows me.

Arjuna, all creatures because of anger and jealousy, because of the dual nature of emotion, experience irrationality.

Those who behave correctly overcome their bad deeds, eliminate dualistic temptations, and with determination worship me.

To get rid of old age and death, they surrender to me and try to know the right knowledge, and know what is to be done.

Those who know this eternal principle present in all the living and non-living, and the basic fire ritual, are settled and with their mind at peace will know me even at the time of their death."

Thus ends the seventh chapter of the Bhagvad Gita, theology, Upanishad and science of yoga in the form of a dialogue between Shri Krishna and Arjuna, called "Dnyan Vidnyan yoga" (Knowledge and Para-Knowledge).

CHAPTER EIGHT

Arjuna said,

"Krishna, what is this Brahman (The Eternal Principle)? Has it got any attributes or not? What is theosophy? What is that which lives in this body? What is an act? What is the basic principle of all creatures?

Tell me about the basic fire ritual. How can we think about it? Is it there in our body? And how do wise people know you at the time of death?"

Shri Bhagvan said,

"The eternal indestructible syllable is the basic principle. When it is in some body it has some basic disposition. The study of this basic disposition is theosophy. The thing one does for others is the basic act.

The basic principle in all the living and non-living is its mutation. The eternal male living in all is the basic God principle. And Arjuna *I am the basic fire ritual* living in all bodies.

One who remembers me at the time of his death, leaves his body and comes to my world. There is no doubt about it.

Arjuna, whatever a person thinks about at the time of death, the person enters that state (because when one thinks about a subject intently, he becomes that subject).

So always think about me. Remember me and battle. As you have dedicated your mind and intellect to me, you will reach my world without any doubt.

To concentrate on me and to make constant practice of that, makes one settled in me and nothing else. Such practice takes you to the heaven where the sun brightly shines.

The wise man who thinks at the time of his death, about the creator and preserver of this universe, microscopic as the atom, the giver of fruits, bright like the sun, beyond all doubts, that is I, reaches me.

At the time of death, one who meditates on the midpoint between the two eyebrows and alertly takes his mind there, reaches that divine being.

Those who know the Vedas call it indestructible; those who have given up their desires enter into that. The knowledge seekers remain celibate and try to know it. I shall tell you Arjuna about that supreme position. This is known as the indesructible God Principle.

Controlling all the doors of knowledge, fixing the mind in the heart, taking the life breath to the top of the head, uttering Om the sacred Word, and then meditating on me, makes one leave his body and come to me, which is the Supreme State.

To the one who has no other interest than God in him, and to the one who always remembers me, I am easily accessible. Those great souls who achieve salvation reach me, and are never subjected to birth which is the root cause of all miseries.

Arjuna, from this visible world to Brahma's world everything moves in cycles again and again, but once you reach me, there are no rebirths.

The wise men know that Brahmadeva's (the creator in the Divine Trinity, Vishnu is the preserver, while Shiva is the destroyer) single day is equal to 1000 times the four yugas. His night is of equivilent magnitude.

When Brahmadeva's day rises, all the world becomes manifest. When Brahmadeva's night rises all the universe merges in to his state, called 'unmanifest'. Arjuna, all this world again and again, merges into Brahmadeva's night and manifests again when Brahmadeva's day rises.

But something different than that unmanifest, which cannot be sensed by the organs, never perishes when the whole universe perishes.

That unmanifest and indestructible is known as the highest state. The state to which one goes, and never returns, is my supreme state. Arjuna, that Supreme Being in whom this entire universe is, and whom has occupied all space, is attainable only through pure devotion.

Arjuna, I shall tell you about the time when the yogis die and reach salvation or are subjected to rebirth.

Agni or fire, proud of time, flame, the deity regulating the daytime, the deity regulating the time when the sun is in the northern hemisphere, are present in the six months called Uttarayana or Northern Path. When the seekers of Brahma leave their bodies during this period, they reach Brahma (when the sun is in Northern sky, the time is called Uttarayana).

The deity of smoke, the night Goddess, the dark moon period Goddess, the deity for the six months when the sun is in the southern hemisphere, are present in the Dakshinayana (the Southern Path). People who die during this period obtain the moon's lot. As long as the reward for the good deeds are there, they enjoy this. After that again they come down. They are reborn.

The people who are guided by knowledge and action have to take these two paths, namely the light path and the dark path. The light path takes you to the supreme state. The dark path takes you back (to the cycle of birth and death).

Arjuna, those who know about these paths are never tempted. So Arjuna, at all time keep your mind settled.

One who meditates, follows what has been told, learns the Vedas, practices the fire rituals, receives the fruits of all these, donations and penance, goes beyond this and reaches the Supreme State."

Thus ends the eighth chapter of the Bhagvad Gita, theology, Upanishad and science of yoga in the form of a dialogue between Shri Krishna and Arjuna, titled "Akshar Brahmayoga" (The Yoga of the Indestructible God Principle).

CHAPTER NINE

Shri Bhagvan said,

"Now I shall tell you about that very secret knowledge, with its science and my experiences, which will liberate you from this illusive life, because you always look upon my finer qualities.

This is the most prominent knowledge, and also the most secret of the secrets. This is very pious, very good, and can be experienced. This is according to the traditions, and can be attained. There are no attachments. The results of this knowledge do not weaken the results of actions.

Arjuna, those who do not believe in this, do not attain me and so have to return to the cycle of life and birth.

I, who am unmanifest, have occupied this whole universe. All creatures are within me, but I am not in them.

Subjectively all creatures are not in me. Look at my Godly nature. I carry them and I nurture them. I am not in them. My nature creates them.

As it is said that wind is everywhere but is settled in the sky, all creatures are settled in me.

At the end of the kalpa (one day and one night of Brahmadeva) all creatures merge in me, and at the beginning I create them again.

These actions Arjuna, do not bind me because I have no desire for them.

Because of my nature which is pure knowledge, my illusion of three qualities creates this universe because of my guiding nature. My guiding nature is the reason behind this world.

Fools who do not recognize me as God regard me, manifest in this human body, as nothing and disobey me.

Their hopes go in vain, their deeds are in vain. Their knowledge is in vain. They lose their reason and they take resort in demonic and tempting nature.

Arjuna, those who are of saintly nature know that I am the reason of all creatures and worship me.

Those who think of me day and night, control their senses and try with all their might. Those who have undertaken decided tasks, they bow before me and worship me in a liberated state.

The knowledge of God is the only knowledge, and is the fire ritual. Those who know this worship me as the almighty God, or thinking that I am the sun, moon or whole universe, worship me in different ways.

I am the fire ritual, I am all other rituals, and I am the offering to the ancestors. I am food as medicine which is consumed by all. I am the sacred utterances (mantras), I am that which is put into the fire ritual and I am that burning process.

I am the father of this universe, and I am the mother. I bestow the fruits of action. I am the grandfather. I am the knowable. I am the purifying water. I am the mono-syllable, Om. I am the *Rigveda*, the *Samveda* and the *Yajurveda*.

I am the fruit of the action, I am the nurturer, I am the master, I am the seer who sees the good deeds and bad deeds of the people. I am the abode of all creatures. I am the cure of the suffering ones who invoke me. I am the friend who helps without expectation. I am the creator, preserver, and destroyer of this universe. I am the store of the fruits of action, and I am the Seed of this universe.

As the sun I generate heat and burn. I stop the rains and I bring the rains. Arjuna, I am ambrosia for the Gods and I am death for the mortals. I am that which manifests through different names.

The people who study the three Vedas, the drinkers of Soma (an intoxicant made of a kind of mushroom), and are also purified, worship me through fire rituals and pray to obtain the heaven where Indra rules and to enjoy the pleasures available to divine beings.

Those Vaidikas (followers of the Vedas) reach to this heaven and live there as long as their good deeds allow them. Once they become weak they are reborn on this earth. Thus the Vaidikas, the ritual followers, those who are desirous of something, are given whatever they want.

I take care of those devotees who become engrossed in me and meditate on me.

Those who worship other deities, also worship me by ignorance (for I am present in all).

Because whatever one offers to the fire is consumed by me, and I am the master. But those who worship the other deities, do not know this in principle, so they don't obtain the desired fruits.

Those who worship other deities go to the heaven where their deities reside. Those that worship the ancestors go to their ancestors. Those who worship the spirits go to that level, and those who worship me come to me.

Arjuna, I accept whatever is offered to me. Though it might be a leaf, a flower, water or some fruit.

Arjuna, whatever you do, whatever you eat, whatever you offer to fire, whatever alms you give and whatever penances you do, offer it all to me.

I see the same in all creatures. Nobody is dear to me and I have no enemies. Those who worship me are with me, and I am with them.

Even if a sinner becomes a devotee of mine and starts worshiping me, he should be considered as a righteous person because he is on the right path.

That righteous person attains eternal peace. Arjuna, my devotee never perishes.

Arjuna, those who take resort in me, women, merchants, the lower caste people, or others born in very low status, enter the highest of states.

The Brahmins and Kshatriyas, the learned among them, will definitely reach that state. So Arjuna, as you are born in this mortal world, worship me.

Keep your mind on me, be my disciple, be my worshiper, bow before me, and then you who are engrossed in me will come to me, who is the soul of everything."

(One has to surrender to God. One need not bother about other methods. In whatever method you worship God, no matter what kind of Mantras you utter, God hears you. This principle is used by Count Lev Tolstoy in his story "The Three Hermits.")

Thus ends the ninth chapter of the Bhagvad Gita, a theology, Upanishad and science of yoga, in the form of a dialogue between Shri Krishna and Arjuna called "Rajvidya Rajguhyayoga" (The Royal Wisdom and Secret Knowledge).

CHAPTER TEN

Shri Bhagvan said,

"Arjuna, listen to me. You are pleased to listen, so I am telling you this for your benefit.

My impact is not known to the highest of Gods. Not even the most learned know anything about me.

The wise man who knows me as unborn, without beginning, and as the Almighty God, is absolved of all his sins.

The intelligence, knowledge, clarity of thinking, controlling the organs, controlling the mind, happiness, sorrow, worldliness and the lack of it, fear and fearlessness, non-violence, equality, satisfaction, penance, giving alms, success, failure - all these qualities in creatures are created by me.

The seven sages, the four before them, the fourteen Manus (the first man is Manu) are the expressions of my mind from whom this entire world is generated.

One who knows about my Godly images through meditation becomes one with me.

I am the reason for the creation of this universe. All the affairs of the world are caused by me. The wise men know this principle, and always worship me with utmost devotion.

Those whose mind is on me and who are ready to die for me, always talk about me among themselves, are delighted in speaking about me, and are engrossed in me.

To such people who are always thinking about me and worship me, I impart that knowledge which finally leads them to me.

To favor them, I myself go into their minds and remove the darkness of ignorance by lighting the lamp of knowledge."

Arjuna said,

"You are the Eternal Principle. You are that final abode. You are very pious. All sages call you the Eternal Divine Being, the God of Gods, the Unborn, and the Omnipresent. The sage Narada, Aasit, the sage Deval, the sage Vyas, and you yourself have said this to me.

Shri Krishna, I regard everything that you say as the gospel truth. Your great persona is known to the demons and divine beings.

O Creator of the Universe, God of Gods, Master of this World, you know your true nature.

You are the right person to tell me about those divine images of yours, through whom you have occupied this world.

O Master of the Yogis, how can I always meditate on you? In what manner can I concentrate on you?

Janardana, tell me about your divine images in detail because your sweet words always leave me unsatisfied, as I want to listen to you more and more."

Shri Bhagvan said,

"I shall tell you about my chief images because my expanse is unending.

Arjuna, I am the life force of all creatures. I am the beginning, the middle, and the end of all creatures.

Among the twelve Adityas (Suns) I am Vishnu. Among the bright flames I am the sun with the rays. Among the Marutas (Winds) I am Marichi. Among the celestial bodies, I am the moon.

Among the Vedas I am the *Samveda*. Among the Gods, I am Indra. Among the organs, I am the mind. I am the life in all creatures.

Among the Rudras, I am Shankara. Among the Yakshas and Rakshasa, I am Kuber (Treasurer of the Gods). Among the eight Vasus, I am Pavak Agni (Fire), and among the peaks I am Meru. (This was supposed to be the highest peak.)

Arjuna, among the priests I am Brahspati (Jupiter). Among the generals I am Skanda (Shiva's son). Among the bodies of water I am the ocean. Among the sages I am Bhrugu. Among the letters I am the monosyllabic Om. Among the fire rituals I am the Japa (recitation of my names). Among the immovable, I am the Himalayas.

Among the trees I am Peepal. Among the sages of the Gods I am Narada. Among the Gandharvas (the celestial beings who are experts in singing) I am Chitraratha. Among the wise and realized beings I am Kapil. Among the horses I am Uchaishrava (a divine horse who came out from the sea when they churned it for the drink of immortality). Among the elephants I am Airawata (the elephant which is in heaven). Among all people, know that the King is I.

Among the weapons I am Vajra (Indra's weapon made of a sage's bones). Among the cows I am Kamdhenu (the celestial cow who fulfills all the wishes). I am the lust which causes the production. Amongst the snakes I am Vasuki. Among the cobras I am Ananta. Among the water deities I am Varuna. Among the ancestors I am Aryama, the king of ancestors. Among the controllers I am Yama (God of death)

Among the demons I am Pralhada. Among the measurements I am time. Among the animals I am the lion. Among the birds I am the eagle.

Among the sanctifiers I am the wind. Among the armed people I am Rama (the earlier incarnation of Vishnu and hero of the epic *Ramayana*). Among the aquatic animals I am the crocodile. Among the rivers I am Ganga.

I am the beginning, middle, and the end of the universe. Among the branches of learning, I am the science of the soul. Among the discussions, I am the debate which draws the final conclusion. Among the letters I am A. Among the compounds I am the binary compound. I am the eternal time. I am the one who decides the fruits of action of this world.

I am the death which takes away life and wealth. I am the cause of prospective progress. Among women I am Kirty (Fame), Shree (Wealth), Vak (Speech), Smruti (Memory) Medha (Higher Form of Intelligence), Dhruti (The Bearing), and Kshama (Forgiving Nature).

In the Samas (from *Samaveda*) I am Bruhat Sam. Among the meters I am Gayatri meter. Among the months I am Margashirsha. Among the seasons I am the spring.

Among the swindlers I am gambling. I am the charisma of the charismatic people. I am the victory of those who are victorious. For the mercantile community I am their merchandise. I am the truth of the truth seekers. Among the Vrushnis, I am Vasudeva Shri Krishna. Among the sons of Pandu I am Arjuna. Among the sages I am Vyasa (the composer of the *Mahabharata*). Among the poets I am Shukracharya (whose composition is not surviving).

I am the penalty of the penalisers. I am the ethics for the seekers of victory. Among the secrets I am silence (keeping mute). I am the wisdom of the wise people.

I am the seed of all creatures, everything that moves or is stationary cannot be without me.

Whenever you see something rich, wealthy, shining or mighty, know that it has come from me.

Arjuna, what can you achieve by knowing this and more? This whole universe is manifest from just one small atom of my nature."

Thus ends the tenth chapter of the Bhagvad Gita, a theology, Upanishad and science of yoga in the form of a dialogue between Shri Krishna and Arjuna called "Vibhutiyoga" (About the Divine Images).

CHAPTER ELEVEN

Arjuna said,

"Krishna, whatever secret knowledge, the science of the soul, you told to bless me has removed my temptations altogether.

O one with lotus eyes, I heard from you that all beings are born of you and finally merge in you. You told it in detail and also conveyed its importance.

O God, as you have told me and as it is, I wish to see the Divine nature of yours.

O Master, if I can see it and if you think that it is possible, show me that great universal form of yours."

Shri Bhagvan said,

"Arjuna, you see my different divine forms, of different colors and of different shape, in their hundreds and thousands.

See the twelve Adityas, eleven Rudras, two Ashwinikumars, the Marutas (forty nine in number), and see the unforeseen wonders.

O conquerer of sleep, see in my body the whole universe with all the creatures, and whatever else you want to see.

You cannot see me with your naked eyes. I shall give you super vision. Witness my divine form."

Sanjay said,

"O King, thus saying, that Master of Yogis Shri Krishna, showed his divine form to Arjuna.

That divine form had many faces and many eyes, many wonderful visions, divine ornaments, and also different kinds of divine weapons.

The God showed Arjuna the universal form in which He was wearing celestial flowers and fragrances, and was immense and endless.

If one thousand suns shine in the sky at the same time, their light may equal the light of that universal being.

Arjuna saw the whole universe in the body of that universal God being.

Then Arjuna, stunned and in awe, bowed before the God and said this with folded hands."

Arjuna said,

"O God, I see in your body all the deities, groups of spirits, Brahma sitting on the lotus, Shankara, all the sages and divine snakes.

O Master of the Universe, I see your many hands, many bellies, many faces, many eyes, unending from all sides, still O Universal being, I see no end, no middle and no beginning.

I see Your crowned head, Your mace and Your chakra (a circular weapon of Vishnu which returned to the sender). You are radiating from all sides, as does the well lit fire and sun, which is very deep and incomparable.

You are that knowable letter. You are the resort of the world. You are the protector of the tradition, and in my opinion You are the eternal being.

You have no beginning, no middle, and no end. You have infinite energy. I see You with Your many hands, the sun and moon are Your eyes. Your face is like a radiant fire and You are scorching this world with Your heat.

From this earth to the sky, all directions are filled by You and all the three worlds are frightened by Your extraordinary and terrible form.

All these groups of deities are entering into You, some are frightened and they are praying with folded hands, reciting Your names and qualities. The sages, and other great souls are saying "Swasti" (let there be good), and praising You with the best of hymns.

The eleven Rudras, twelve Adityas, eight Vasus, the Sadhyas, Vishwedeva Ashwinikumar, Marutas, the ancestors, Gandharvas, Yakshas, Rakshasas, and the realized souls are looking at You in amazement.

Krishna, this form of Yours is terrible. There are many faces and eyes, many hands, thighs and feet, and many bellies. It all looks fearsome because of the teeth. All the people are frightened. I am also disturbed.

O all occupying God, You are touching the sky with opened mouths. The radiance has many colors. Your eyes are glaring and very big. Looking at You I am frightened, and my peace of my mind is gone.

When I look at Your terrible teeth like the great fire, I don't know the directions, I am not happy. So God, the Shelter of this world bless me.

All the kings, Dhrutarashtra's sons, grandfather Bhishma, our master Drona, our main warriors, the son of Suta, Karna all are entering into You.

They are entering Your mouth to be devoured. I see many of them stuck in the gaps between your teeth with crushed skulls.

As the rivers rush in the sea via many streams, these warriors are entering Your radiant mouth.

As the insects jump into the fire, these warriors are speedily entering Your mouth to perish.

O God, You are swallowing these people with your blazing mouth, and this terrible light is bringing woe to the world.

Tell me, who are You of this terrible form? I bow before You. Almighty God bless me. You are the chief reason for this universe and I want to know You, because I cannot understand Your game."

Shri Bhagvan said,

"I am the annihilator of people and I have grown at large. I am going to kill these people. The warriors present here will all disappear without you (even if you do not kill them). So rise to victory. Conquer these enemies and enjoy the wealth of the kingdom. These warriors have already been killed by me, so you will be here only for namesake. Kill Drona, Bhishma, Jaydratha, Karna and the other warriors whom I have already killed. Do not grieve. Do not be afraid of them. Fight with them and you will conquer them in the battle.

(The second person is God so the capital Y is used.)

Sanjay said,

"When Arjuna, who was shivering and frightened, heard Shri Krishna saying this he folded his hands, saluted Shri Krishna and spoke in a stuttering and choking voice."

Arjuna said,

"Shri Krishna, when they hear about You the whole universe is pleased, they fall in for You, love You, and this is right. The Rakshasas are frightened and are fleeing. The realized beings bow before You, and that too is right.

And why would they not bow before You, who is the beginning and the maker or the creator?

O unending, manifest in the universe, You are the supreme principle and one that is not there. You are that Word.

You are the God, that ancient being. You are the last resort of this universe. There is no end to You. You have occupied the whole universe.

You are the wind, Yama, Varuna, the Moon, Prajapati, the father of Brahmadeva.

I bow before You a thousand times. I bow before You from the East and from the West. I bow before You who are present in all directions, whose might is limitless. You have occupied the whole world. Everything is You.

Because of ignorance about Your universal nature, or because of love or by mistake I regarded you as my equal, as my friend and called you Krishna Yadava or friend.

And, either in fun, when we sat together, dined together or took rest together, I might have insulted You, so please forgive my indolence.

You are the father of this universe. You are the Master of masters so You deserve more reverence. There is none like You in all the three worlds, how can there be?

So my Lord, I fall at Your feet, salute You, pray and ask for your blessings. As the father forgives his son, as a friend forgives his friend, as a husband forgives his dear wife, my offenses can be overlooked by You.

This wonderful form of Yours was not seen by me in the past, so I am pleased, amazed, and also frightened by looking at You. I now long to see you in your normal form, so please have mercy.

I want to see you again with your crown, mace, and chakra, so please o God, please come back to your normal form."

(Actually Krishna had promised that he would not fight in the battle so he remained without any arms till the end.)

Shri Bhagvan said,

"Arjuna, I am pleased with you, this form I have shown to you as my immense and unlimited form has been seen by none before you.

Arjuna, in this mortal world nobody can see this universal form even if they study the Vedas, perform fire rituals, yogic actions, or do penance.

As I want you to not be frightened or lose your senses because of my terrible form, look at my normal form with the conch, mace and chakra."

Sanjay said,

"Vasudeva (Shri Krishna) said this to Arjuna, appeared in his normal form with four hands, was very calm and consoled the frightened Arjuna."

Arjuna said,

"O Lord, I have become very calm and I am my normal self after looking at your peaceful human form."

Shri Bhagvan said,

"Arjuna, this form of mine with four hands is also difficult to see, even the Gods yearn to see this form.

No study of Veda, no penance, giving alms, nor fire ritual can entitle anyone to see this form of mine with four hands which you have seen.

Arjuna, by devotion, one can see me, know me, enter into me, or be one with me.

So one who does his duties for me, has the sole objective of achieving me, is my devotee and listens to me, thinks about me and without any other desire, renounces everything, and looks at all creatures equally without affection or enmity, finally comes to me."

Thus ends the eleventh chapter of the Bhagvad Gita, theology, Upanishad and science of yoga in the form of a dialogue between Shri Krishna and Arjuna, called "Vishwarupa Darshans Yoga" (The Vision of God as Universe).

CHAPTER TWELVE

Arjuna said,

"There are some who are engaged in worshiping you day and night. They do all the rituals, meditate on you, are either slow or medium paced in their devotion, and there are some who worship the formless God. Who is superior amongst them?"

Shri Bhagvan said,

"Those who worship me in form and think of me as manifest in all the universe, and meditate on my qualities are my best devotees. I regard worshiping formed God superior to worshiping formless God.

But those who look at everything equally and think of their interests, control their sense organs and meditate on That which is abstract, which cannot be named, which is in the whole universe, which has no ripples, which is immovable, which is Word, day and night, finally come to me.

Those who are attracted towards formless God have to suffer more than those who are worshiping formed God, because if one thinks of his body as his, worshiping and attaining formless god is very difficult, so worshiping formed is better than formless.

Arjuna, those who have their mind on me are absolved from this mortal world very soon by me.

Fix your mind in me. Think of me as a formed God manifest in the universe. Your reason should decidedly be in me. If your mind and reason remain in me after your death, you will also remain in me. There is no doubt about that.

If you cannot fix your mind on me, do practice, control your mind and try to fix it on me.

If even that practice is not possible, do all your duties for me. Think that you are doing everything for me. If you do your duties for me, finally you will reach me.

If even that is not possible, dedicate all your actions to me. You do them, but dedicate them to me. Control your mind and give up all the fruits of action.

Knowledge is superior to practice, this is well known. Meditation with knowledge is still better. If you can give up the fruits of actions after knowledge, it is even better. The mortals are happy and calm only when they give up the fruits of action.

One who looks at all beings equally, has no enmity, loves all selflessly, is kind without any vested interest, has no ego, and regards happiness and sorrow as the same and forgives all, is very dear to me.

My devotee who is content and meditates on me with his mind and body under control, has full faith in me, who has surrendered everything to me, is very dear to me.

My devotee who never causes any trouble to others or to one whom none can cause trouble, who has no fear, no joy, and no jealousy, is very dear to me.

My devotee who has no expectations, is pious within and without, has completed the mission for which he has come, is neutral, has no sorrows, and has given up all beginnings, is very dear to me.

My disciple who never has any delight, knows no jealousy, never mourns, and never desires, one who has given up the fruits of all good and bad actions, is very dear to me.

One who regards enemies and friends as the same, for whom honor and insult are the same, one who treats heat and cold, happiness and sorrow as the same, and one who has no desires, is very dear to me.

One for whom criticism and flattery is the same, one who keeps quiet, is content in whatever he gets and settled in mind, that devotee is very dear to me.

Those faithful devotees, who drink the ambrosia of the tradition, are very dear to me."

Thus ends the twelfth chapter of the Bhagvad Gita, theology, Upanishad and science of yoga in the form of a dialogue between Shri Krishna and Arjuna called "Bhaktiyoga" (Devotion).

CHAPTER THIRTEEN

Shri Bhagvan said,

"Arjuna, this body is called a field and one who knows that is called the knower of field.

And one who lives in this field is the knower of field, and that is I. I think that the knowledge about this field and the knower of the field is the supreme knowledge.

What is that field? What is its type? What are the different attributes? What are its jobs, with what reason? Who is the knower of the field? How is he affected? Listen to me for the answers in brief.

This is sung by the sages in different meters, logically and decidedly in the *Brahmasutras* (One classic scripture).

The five elements, the self, the intelligence,the eleven organs, the desire to enjoy through the organs, hatred, happiness, sorrow, the whole body and the mind in that body with its attributes, is called the field.

To be unassuming, to be without pride, to be non-violent, to be very calm, serving the masters (spiritual teachers), keeping the mind and body clean, with determined nature, with perfect control of

73

one's body, the renunciation of sensual pleasures, with humbleness, and thinking about birth, illness and death, dislike of senses, not being too involved with wife and children, remaining neutral about the good or bad, these are all ways of gaining knowledge.

Full hearted devotion, living in solitude, sacred places, not liking crowds, are also ways of gaining knowledge.

To think constantly about the soul and the material, and to think about philosophical ideas, these are the gateways to knowledge, the opposite of which is ignorance.

I shall tell you what is knowable, knowing that you will become immortal. One which has no beginning is that God Principle, is knowable, and is neither called sat nor asat (true or untrue).

The knowable has hands and feet on all sides, eyes, heads and faces on all sides, ears on all sides. The God Principle is occupying all spaces, things, and creatures.

All senses can feel it, but it is devoid of organs so it is uninterested in anything, yet it carries all and is the base of everything. There are no attributes of it, yet it enjoys happiness, sorrow, and temptations.

It is within all creatures. It is stationary and mobile. This knowable is so minute that it becomes unknowable and remote, but for believers it is near to their heart.

It is inseparable from the bodies of creatures but remains separate. It appears to be different in every body. At the time of their existence, this knowable takes care of their body (is responsible for their existence). In the end it destroys them and in the beginning it manifests them.

That knowable is the light of the sun and the fire. It gives light to light. Ignorance cannot touch It. Knowledge, the knowable and the effect of knowledge is trifold, and is settled in the minds of all creatures.

I have told you in brief about the field, knowledge, and the knowable God principle. My devotee, who thinks only about me, knows all and finally comes to me.

There are eight kinds of natures, and the one who resides in the body is without any beginning and is eternal. Know that all attributes of the body, mind, sense organs, and all the feelings are generated from my three attributive illusions.

Action and cause are of this nature, the soul residing in the body is the reason to enjoy happiness and sorrow.

The soul residing in the body because of bodily attachments thinks of himself as the body and enjoys happiness or sorrow. Because of this and the various attributes of the body, he is born again and again in different forms. That is the reason.

One who looks at things closely and supports, nurtures, and consumes, is called God and is the one residing in this body (Field).

If one knows about this being who lives in the body with all the attributes, that fellow is not born again, no matter how he behaves.

Some yogis meditate and see this soul. Even with an egalitarian view it can be seen, and it can also be seen by dedicating all your actions to God.

Besides these solutions, some listen to other masters who tell them that those who think, meditate, and worship devotedly are also saved from this cycle of life and death.

Arjuna, whatever movable and immovable force is present, is a result of the conjoining of the field and the knower of the field. If one sees the Eternal God in all mortal things, he sees the correct thing.

For if you see God everywhere, then you cannot kill yourself and reach that supreme state. If one sees that all actions are from the illusive body of the God, and sees the soul as the non-doer, he sees correctly.

If one sees that the difference of all the creatures is in one soul and sees God expanded in all universes, he becomes God.

This supreme soul, because it has no beginning and has no attributes, is indestructible. Arjuna, this soul residing in the body never does anything, and is not affected by the effects of action.

As the horizon, because of its endlessness, is not affected by anything, this soul which is in all bodies is not affected by the actions of the body.

As the sun gives light to the whole universe, this knower of the field, the soul, gives light to the whole field, the body.

If one sees the difference between the field and the knower of the field, how can creatures reach salvation with knowledge through their enlightened vision to reach the final supreme state?"

Thus ends the thirteenth chapter of the Bhagvad Gita, theology Upanishad, and science of yoga in the form of a dialogue between Shri Krishna and Arjuna, called Kshetrakshetradnyayoga (About the Field (body) and the knower of the Field (the soul)).

CHAPTER FOURTEEN

Shri Bhagvan said,

I shall give you the best of knowledge, after knowing that the wise men have reached the supreme state after their death.

Those who have this knowledge and attain me are never born at the time of genesis or destroyed at the time of the end.

My female nature is the cause of all beings. She is the Supreme Being as she is greater than anything and knows all her aspects. I impregnate her and all creatures are born.

All the creatures of different types who come into being are born of my female nature. I sow the seed, so I am the father.

Arjuna, satwa (goodness) raja (moderate) and tama (wickedness) are the three qualities that bind the soul to the body.

Goodness is the shining one and because of its pious nature, it binds the person with desire for happiness and knowledge.

Moderateness is born of desire and attraction, so it binds the person to deeds with the desire for fruits.

Wickedness is born of ignorance, so it binds the people with offenses, laziness, and sleep.

The good people are engaged in happiness, the moderates in actions, while wickedness obscures knowledge and leads the people to offenses.

Arjuna, goodness overcomes moderateness and wickedness, the wickedness overcomes the moderateness and goodness, the moderateness overcomes goodness and wickedness.

When the body and mind are enlightened and there is wisdom, know that goodness is on the rise.

When the moderateness increases, the person has desires, worldly affairs, and starts to do things with selfish interests. The mind is in unrest, and the person wants to enjoy all worldly pleasures.

When the wickedness rises, there is darkness in the mind. The person does not want to do his duties and so commits offenses, whilst greed and other evil tendencies are born.

If one dies when the goodness is on the rise, because of his good deeds he reaches the heaven which is very clean.

If one dies when moderateness is on the rise, he is born amongst those who want to do deeds, and if one dies when wickedness is on the rise, he is born amongst the lower dumb animals.

The fruits of good actions are good like happiness, knowledge and renunciation; the moderate actions bring unhappiness, and the wicked actions breed ignorance.

Goodness breeds knowledge, moderateness breeds greed, and wickedness breeds offenses, temptations, and ignorance.

The people who are good go to higher worlds, moderates are born again amongst men, and the wicked go to the lower categories.

When one understands that these three qualities are the doers and knows me who am beyond these three qualities, he comes to me.

One who goes beyond these three qualities and the reason of the mortal body, he gets rid of birth, death, old age, all other sorrows and receives supreme bliss."

Arjuna said,

"What are the traits of the people with these three qualities? How do they behave? How can one go beyond these three qualities?"

Shri Bhagvan said,

"One who sees the light of goodness, the action of moderateness and the temptations of wickedness, does not think of them as bad or does not seek them once he is out of them.

He is neutral, he cannot be moved and knows that the qualities are the doers and concentrates on God, and so is not moved from that state.

One absorbed in the self regards happiness and sorrow as the same, gold and dust as the same, is courageous, for whom likes and dislikes are the same, and for whom criticism and flattery are the same.

Honor and insult are the same to him. Friends and enemies are the same. He has given up all beginnings. Such a person is beyond all qualities.

And he, who worships me with sheer devotion, can go beyond all the qualities and can become one with the God Principle."

Thus ends the fourteenth chapter of the Bhagvad Gita, theology, Upanishad and science of yoga, in the form of a dialogue between Shri Krishna and Arjuna, called "Guntrayavibhag Yoga" (Division of the Three Qualities).

CHAPTER FIFTEEN

Shri Bhagvan said,

"Arjuna, this God Principle is like a peeple tree, whose roots are up and the branches are down. The Vedas are its leaves. If one knows about this, he gets the summary of the Vedas.

The branches of this tree, nurtured by the three qualities are spread down. The different objects of pleasure in human beings and other celestial beings are these branches. The ego affection and relative action bound branches are spread all over the world. (This is the meaning given by Shankaracharya.)

This tree cannot be seen as it is described, because there is no beginning or end to it. It is not settled also. So one has to cut the branches of affection, temptation, etc. with the weapon of renunciation.

And one has to try to seek God. It is that state from where you never return. You should decide that this universal tree has sprung from God and that you surrender totally.

One for whom pride is totally absent, temptations are conquered, desires are won, and whose mind is on God, who is free from the duality called happiness and sorrow, reaches that eternal state.

Sun cannot give light to that, no moon is either. No fire can give light. That supreme abode to which when one goes, but never comes back, is my abode.

The soul living in the body is a fraction of my self, which attracts the five sense organs, with mind dwelling in my three aspects of illusion.

As the wind gets fragrance from its base, the soul leaves one body and takes his mind into the new body that he receives.

This soul enjoys the pleasures with the ears, eyes, skin, tongue, nose and mind.

The ignorant do not know about this soul which leaves the body, or the soul in the body enjoying pleasures. Those who have the eyes of knowledge know it.

The yogis try to know this soul living in the heart. The ignorant cannot know even after trying.

The light that comes from the sun to brighten the whole world, the light from the moon, or the radiance of the fire, is my radiance.

I enter the earth and carry all animals with my might. And then I become the moon which secretes the nectar of immortality, and nurture all the medicine and the vegetation of this world.

I become the fire called Vaishvanara, living in the body of the animals and digest four types of food with incoming and out going breath.

I live in the hearts of all - memory, knowledge, and reasoning are given by me. All Vedas try to know me. The creator of Vedanta and the knower of Vedas are me.

The best man is one who occupies the three worlds and takes care of all, and is called God.

Because I am beyond all perishable things, I am greater than the imperishable soul so I am called "Purushottama" (Best Man) by the Vedas.

Arjuna, who knows me as Purushottama, that all knowing being worships me in all the ways.

Arjuna, this most confidential knowledge is given by me, knowing that the learned become immensely satisfied."

Thus ends the fifteenth chapter of the Bhagvad Gita, theology, Upanishad and science of yoga in the form of a dialogue between Shri Krishna and Arjuna, called "Purushottama Yoga" (About the Best Man).

CHAPTER SIXTEEN

Shri Bhagvan said,

"To be fearless, to have a clean mind, to be determined to know, giving alms to the right people, to conquer the senses, to perform the fire ritual, to recite and remember the God, to do penance, to be humble, to be nonviolent, to be of sweet tongue, to be without anger, to have renunciated, to be peaceful, to be uncriticizing, to be kind towards all living beings, to have no greed, to be tender, to be ashamed of going against traditions, to be devoid of trivial actions, to have radiance, to be forgiving, to be courageous, to have no enmity with anybody, to be without pride - these are the qualities of a man who possesses divine wealth.

Arjuna, hypocrisy, pride, ego, anger, acid tongue, and ignorance - these are the qualities of a man who possesses demonic wealth.

Divine wealth leads to liberation and demonic wealth leads to bondage, but Arjuna, you don't have to worry because you have divine wealth.

Arjuna, there are two kinds of dispositions in this world. One is like the divine being and the other is like the demons. Now I have explained about the divine beings in detail, so listen as I explain the demonic disposition in detail.

The men with demonic qualities do not know to turn towards their duties or to turn away from the avoidable, so they are neither clean inside, nor is their behavior right. There is no truth in their utterances.

Those with demonic qualities say that there is no power behind this universe, everything here is a lie, and there is no God. According to them this world has come into existence because of the copulation of the sexes so it is there only to enjoy. They ask "what else is there?"

Those who have resorted to this baseless knowledge are lost and these idiots, who are treacherous and cruel, are born only to destroy this world.

These hypocrites, who have false pride and harbor desires which are never fulfilled, ignorantly follow false principles, and go on behaving in a fallen way.

They have infinite worries which last till their death, and they go on living a lustful life thinking that this is the only bliss.

Hundreds of hopes bind them and involve them in lust and anger, to fulfill their passion, they unjustly try to store wealth etc.

(They think) "Today I have this, and this desire of mine is fulfilled. Today I have this much money. Tomorrow I shall have this much.

I killed that enemy. I shall finish my other enemies. I am God and I enjoy everything. I have all the powers. I am mighty and happy.

I am wealthy. I have a big family. There is nobody like me. I shall conduct the fire ritual, give alms, and shall be delighted. And they are tempted by such ignorance."

They are drawn towards many ideas which go on confusing them, and these ignorant men engaged in lustful activities, finally go to the dirtiest hell.

These proud men who think very highly about themselves, conduct the fire ritual without proper procedure, reciting the names blasphemously.

Those engaged in ego, might and anger, and always criticizing others, hate me who lives in them and others.

Those haters of me, who are sinners, evil and wicked, and are the worst of men, I send them back to this planet again and again in demonic lives.

Arjuna, these idiots are born demonic again and again, and the demons because they are unable to attain me, they reach the lowest state that is hell.

Lust, anger, and greed are the gates of three hells that are the destroyers which cause the downfall, so one has to reject them.

Arjuna, those who give up these three gates, think of this and finally reach me.

Those who are not following the scriptures, and follow their own methods, neither gain a higher state nor happiness.

So for you duties and that which is avoidable are prescribed in the scriptures. Know that you are to do whatever the scriptures prescribe."

Thus ends the sixteenth chapter of the Bhagvad Gita, theology and Upanishad and science of yoga in the form of a dialogue between Shri Krishna and Arjuna called "Daivasursampadvibhagyoga" (The Division of Divine and Demonic Wealth).

CHAPTER SEVENTEEN

Arjuna said,

"Krishna, what is the state of those who do not follow any scriptures but worship with full faith? Are they good, moderate, or evil?"

Shri Bhagvan said,

"The faith, which is not following scriptures, but has come naturally, is also of three types. Satwik, Rajsik, and Tamasik (good, moderate, and evil). Listen to me speak about them.

The faith of the man is true to his nature. So the man has faith as his nature is.

Those who are Satwik or good natured, worship the divine beings. The Rajasik or moderate worship Yakshas and Rakshasas. The Tamasik or evil natured worship dead bodies and ghosts.

Those who do not follow scriptures and do very difficult penance on their own have hypocrisy, ego, lust and pride in their strength.

And they weaken the five elements in the body and me, who lives in the mind. Know that such people are Tamasik (evil).

The food is also of three types which are dear to people according to their nature. The fire rituals, penance, and alms is also of three types. Listen about their difference.

The food that increases life span, power, health and love, is juicy and stringy. It remains in the body for a long time, such lovable food is dear to Satwik (good) people.

The food which is bitter, salty, hot, intense, dry and agitating, gives birth to sorrow, worry, and ailment is dear to Rajasik (moderate) people.

The food that is half cooked, is without any juice, is stinking and stale, is tasted by others and is impious, is dear to Tamasik (evil) people.

The fire ritual, performed as told in the scriptures, and with satisfaction without desiring any fruits, is Satwik.

The fire ritual done hypocritically, or with a desire for fruits, know that to be Rajasik (moderate).

The fire ritual performed without any scriptural methods, without any mantras, without giving food and alms, and without any faith is called Tamasik (evil).

Worshiping the Gods, the priests and the learned men, after observing celibacy and non-violence, is called the penance of the body.

The speech which does not agitate anyone, is very precious, is in the interests of the others, is truthful, is about the study of Vedas, and recitation of the names of God, is the penance of the speech.

A pleasing mind and peaceful thinking about God, with control of the mind and pious heart, is called the penance of the mind.

Those not desirous of fruits, the good yogis, do these three kinds of penances which are called Satwik (good).

The penances performed to show false pride and to get felicitation, respect and worship from others, which are not decided and have temporary fruits, are Rajasik penances.

The penances done foolishly, with insistence, by giving a lot of pain to the mind, speech, body or to do harm to others are called Tamasik (evil).

The alms given as a duty, after considering, the place, time and the eligibility of the person without expecting anything in return, is called Satwik alms.

The alms given with a lot of pain, expecting something in return, or with a desire for fruits is called Rajasik alms.

The alms given without felicitation, with hatred at the wrong time and to the wrong person is called Tamasik (evil) alms.

The God Principle which is called by three types as Om Tat Sat, has composed the Brahmanas (the philosophy books), Vedas and the fire ritual from the beginning.

So those who recite the Vedas begin their fire ritual, alms and penances, start their rituals in accordance to the scriptures with Om.

Those desirous of salvation think that all these things belong to Tat (God) and without expecting any fruits perform their fire rituals, do penance and give alms.

Sat is used truthfully and reverentially, Arjuna, even in good actions the word Sat is used.

The state of fire ritual, penance, and giving alms is also Sat. So they say. And the action of God is also called Sat."

Thus ends the seventeenth chapter of the Bhagvad Gita, theology, Upanishad and science of yoga, in the form of a dialogue between Shri Krishna and Arjuna, called "Shraddhatrayavibhagyoga" (The Division of Three Kinds of Faith).

CHAPTER EIGHTEEN

Arjuna said,

"Krishna, I want to know separately about renunciation and giving up."

Shri Bhagvan said,

"According to the learned people, the giving up of actions is renunciation, and many learned people say that when you give up the fruits of action, you really give up.

The learned people say that all acts have vices in them, so they are worth giving up, but some others say that acts like charity and penance are not to be given up.

Arjuna, listen to my opinion about giving up. There are three kinds of giving up.

One should not give up fire sacrifice, charity, and penance because these three are obligatory. There is no doubt about that. Fire sacrifice, charity, and penance purify the wise people.

All these and other acts should be done after giving up the desire of the fruits of action. This is my opinion.

It is not right to give up the assigned acts. Giving them up due to temptation is called the dark giving up (Tamasik).

If one gives up all acts with the assumption that all these are sorrowful and may cause physical pains, this is the moderate giving up (Rajasik) and one who gives up like that is not at all benefited.

Arjuna, if one performs the acts as a duty assigned by the scriptures and does them without any attachment, and gives up the desire for fruits, it is called the virtuous (Satwik) giving up.

One who neither hates the harmful acts, nor is attached to the good acts, is a virtuous and learned man of renunciation. There is no doubt about that.

One who has a body cannot give up all the acts (to maintain the body one has to take care of it and perform some acts). That is why it is said that one who gives up the desire for fruits is a real sacrificer.

Those who have desires, have three kinds of fruits of their acts. They are good, bad, or mixed and this continues even after their deaths. Those who give up their desire for fruits, never have any kind of fruits of their actions.

Arjuna, in Sankhya philosophy, five reasons are given for the fulfillment of every act. Know them clearly from me.

The four reasons are the base, the doer, the different reasons and the attempts to perform the act. There is the fifth reason of destiny.

Whatever a human being does by his mind, body and speech, either according to the scriptures or against the scriptures, is because of these five reasons.

Even then, one who because of an impure mind, sees the pure soul as the doer is not looking right.

One who does not have the attitude that I do and does not have any attachment, either with the things in the world or the acts, may kill all but in reality does not kill and is not tied to any sin.

Knower, knowledge, and knowable are the motivation of all acts (when the three meet, one has the desire to act). Doer, reason and action, are the stores of acts (these three combined make the acts).

Knowledge, act, and doer are of three types because of their qualities according to Sankhya philosophy. Listen about them.

Knowledge that enables us to see the same eternal God principle in different beings is called the good (Satwik) knowledge.

Knowledge that enables us to see different entities in different beings is the middle (Rajasik) knowledge.

And knowledge that makes one attached to his body, and in which there is no reason and no meaning is dark (Tamasik) knowledge.

An act done according to the scriptures, without any assumption, without any desire, without any affection or hatred is a good (Satwik) act.

An act done with great difficulty, with desire for fruits and pride of doing is called the middle (Rajasik) act.

An act done without any thought to its consequence, without considering the harm and violence involved, and the might of the doer is a dark (Tamasik) act.

One who has no attachments, who does not speak proudly, is courageous and enthusiastic and is not affected either by the good or bad results, is called a good (Satwik) doer.

One who has attachments, has a desire for fruits, is greedy, violent, impure, and has emotions like joy and sorrow is a middle (Rajasik) doer.

One whose mind is not right, who is uneducated, proud, cunning, destructive, always sad, lazy and who takes a long time to finish a small job is a dark (Tamasik) doer.

Arjuna, listen to the difference between the three kinds of intelligence and bearing because of the qualities.

The intelligence that knows worldliness and renunciation, the duties and the avoidable, fear and fearlessness, the ties and the freedom, in principle is a good (Satwik) intelligence.

Arjuna, the intelligence that cannot differentiate between right and wrong, duties and avoidable rightly, is the middle one (Rajasik).

Arjuna, the intelligence covered by dark qualities, decides wrong as the right thing, and finds exactly the opposite meaning in everything is a dark intelligence (Tamasik).

The bearing of the yogi who bears his mind, body, and breath in a controlled and pure way is good (Satwik).

The bearing that desires fruit and finds out the meaning of right according to one's interest is the middle one (Rajasik).

Arjuna, the bearing of dark (Tamasik) people is false pride. They are lazy, they are dreaming, are sad, and have all kinds of vices.

Arjuna, even the joys are of three kinds. When an experience removes all sorrows from one's mind, and which in the beginning is like poison, but the effects of which are like nectar, becomes a good (Satwik) joy born after understanding oneself and is a blessing.

When one is experiencing joy after the contact of the body organs with the desired objects, it is a middle (Rajasik) joy which is like nectar in the beginning, but like poison in the end.

The joy experienced in sleep, laziness, intoxicants and committing follies is a dark (Tamasik) joy which is deceptive in the beginning and in the end also.

There is nobody in this world nor among the heavenly beings, that is free from these three qualities which are natural.

The duties of Brahmins (priests), Kshatryas (warriors), Vaishyas (merchants), and Shudras (serving class) have been classified according to their natural qualities and disposition.

The Brahmins have to keep control of their organs and do penance. They have to be pure, clean, and of a forgiving nature. They have to be speakers of truth and should seek knowledge and para-knowledge.

The Kshatriyas are brave, bright, bold and capable. They never run away from the battlefield. They have generosity and are dominating in nature.

The Vaishyas are agriculturists. They maintain cattle and are engaged in trade. The Shudras are engaged in all kinds of service.

If one is doing one's duty devotedly, one attains grand success. Listen to how this can be achieved.

One has to be as his disposition is, and by doing all duties as an offering to the God principle, one attains grand success.

Doing one's duty even though it is not up to the mark is better than doing another's duty perfectly. Do your duty as your nature allows and there is no sin in that.

Arjuna, one should not give up one's duty. In the beginning everything is like fire covered by smoke (once you come to know about it, you can do better).

One who has no attachments anywhere, who has conquered his organs, and who has no desire, realizes the God principle through his renunciation.

Arjuna, listen to how this realization of God is reached and how it is also supreme knowledge.

One has to have a pure intellect, and perfect control over the body and mind. One has to reject every desire including the sounds. One should not have any attachment or any kind of jealousy.

One has to remain in solitude. One has to eat the minimum. He has to have perfect control over his body and mind. One has to meditate and do yoga. One has to renounce everything.

One has to give up ego, adamancy, pride, desire, anger, all of the amassed things, which makes him free and calm, and takes one to the God principle.

One who has become one with the God principle is in a blessed state and he does not grieve nor has any desire. He looks at all beings equally and finally attains the God state.

Because of his devotion he knows me as what I am, and he gives up his body to enter me.

One who performs all his acts with me (the God) in his mind, and surrenders to me, reaches that eternal state through my blessings.

Know me by yoga of knowledge, dedicate all your acts to me, accept me as the Supreme Being and constantly think about me.

If you fix your mind on me, you will conquer all obstacles through my grace. If you refuse due to ego, you will perish.

If you say, "I shall not fight" due to ego, it is of no use. Your nature will make you fight.

You are bound to do things according to your inborn instincts. Arjuna, you are helpless in this matter. You will do the things you do, not want to do.

Arjuna, God resides in the heart of all beings and revolves them like an object mounted on a machine.

Surrender to him Arjuna, and through His grace achieve great peace in that eternal state.

I have conveyed knowledge to you which is very secret. Think on that and do whatever you wish.

Listen to what I am saying. This is a well kept secret. I am telling this to you because you are very dear to me.

Fix your mind on me. Be my devotee. Bow down to me. You will come to me in the end. This is my true promise, because you are very dear to me.

Give up all rituals, surrender to me, and I shall absolve you from all sins. You will not grieve.

This knowledge should never be given to anyone who does not do penance, is not a devotee, does not offer any services to me and who thinks ill of me.

One who is my devotee will pass this ultimate knowledge to my other devotees, and will finally come to me. There is no doubt about that.

That devotee would do better than all others and none will be dearer to me than him.

One who studies this sacred conversation between us, would be worshiping me through the fire sacrifice in the form of knowledge.

This is my opinion.

Anyone who listens to this with devotion, without any doubt will be absolved and will reach the blessed world attainable to the noble souls.

Have you listened to this Arjuna with concentration? Is the delusion caused by ignorance totally gone?"

Arjuna said,

"Krishna, the delusion is destroyed. Now I have my memory back. It is all because of your grace. Now that my doubts are cleared, I shall follow your instructions."

Sanjay said,

"Thus I heard the wonderful conversation between Shri Krishna and Arjuna. Even now it gives me goose pimples.

Because of the blessings of Vyasa (the great sage and composer of the *Mahabharata*), I could hear Shri Krisna, the Lord of the Yogis speaking on the secret yoga.

O King, I remember this sacred dialogue between Krishna and Arjuna again and again, and it gives me great joy.

O King, I remember the great form shown by Shri Krishna (chapter eleven) which was stunning, and it brings me great joy.

Wherever Krishna, the Lord of the Yogis is there, wherever Arjuna the great archer is there, prosperity and victory will be there. I am convinced of that."

Thus ends the eighteenth chapter of the Bhagvad Gita, which is an Upanishad, theology, and science of yoga in the form of a dialogue between Krishna and Arjuna, titled "Mokshasanyasyoga" (The Yoga of Salvation and Renunciation).

THE NAMES OF KRISHNA AND ARJUNA IN THE BHAGVAD GITA

Krishna is referred to as Bhagvan throughout the text. This is how God and godlike people are addressed.

Madhava and Madhusudan are Krishna's names. Both mean "Killer of Madhu, the Demon".

Govind is a name of Krishna, which means the "Maintainer of Cows". Gopal is another name, which does not appear in the Gita.

Janardana is a name of Krishna which means the "Saver or Liberator of People".

Rishikesha is also Krishna's name which means "Master of the Senses".

Krishna is called Yadava because he belonged to the clan of Yadus.

He is also called Varshneya because he belonged to the sub-clan of Vrushnis.

Krishna is known as Vaasudeva because he was the son of Vasudeva.

Krishna is Keshava as he had killed a demon called Keshi.

Krishna is also called Hari which has multiple meanings.

Arjuna is called Bharat, or Bhatarshabh because he belonged to the clan of Bharatas.

He is called Pandava because he was a son of Pandu.

Arjuna is also called Parth, after his mother whose name was Prutha.

Arjuna is called Kaunteya because he was a son of Kunti.

He is called Mahabahu because he had big hands and was a brave warrior.

Arjuna is called Parantapa because he had done great penance.

He is named as Gudakesha because he had conquered sleep.

He is called Dhananjaya because he had conquered wealth.

CONCLUSION

The Gita throws light on many ideologies.

Karmayoga: Everyone is assigned some duties. They cannot be avoided. The other pasture may look greener, but your pasture is important. Do your duties. Don't think about the outcome.

Sankhyayoga: Regard all things as equal. The whole universe is a manifestation of God.

Bhaktiyoga: Recite the names of God. Do your duties. Do not expect fruits. Surrender.

Hathyoga: Through physical exercises, purify your body and awaken the God Principle in you. Leave the rest to God.

There are three qualities in all the beings. One can be Godly, demonic, or animal. The choice rests on him or her.

All paths lead to God.

The God is present in everybody.

There are many planes on which different kinds of beings live.

One becomes what one thinks.

As Krishna says, we have to determine our course and follow it with determination. We have to do our duties without fail. Escapism has no place in the Gita.

This is the secret of the Gita.

ABOUT THE AUTHOR

Raghupati Bhatt belongs to Karnataka, Maharashtra, and Goa. He was born in Karnataka, was brought up in Maharashtra, and he chose Goa as his permanent residence. He taught English in G.V.M's College of Commerce in Ponda, Goa. He contributes regularly to Marathi and English journals. He was awarded "Shiksha Rattan" in 2013. He lives in Ponda with his wife, Vijaya.

The *Bhagvad Gita* is his tenth book.